Tragic Beginnings to Fairytale Endings

Dreams Really Do Come True

Kim Constantineau

Teamwork Makes a Dream Work

PAGE PUBLISHING
Conneaut Lake, PA

First originally published by Page Publishing 2023

ISBN 979-8-88654-259-2 (pbk)
ISBN 979-8-88654-260-8 (digital)

Printed in the United States of America

I dedicate this book to all the wounded and hurting people in this world, to God, and to my beloved daughter whose unconditional love lit a passion in me to give a better life than the one I had.

I gave all the journals that I wrote throughout my dysfunctional childhood to KJ DePontes. These were filled with pain, chaos, and confusion. KJ took those journals and created a roadmap, documenting my experiences as a broken, damaged little girl with *no hope* to the hopeful, happy and thankful woman who God stepped in and rescued.

To be successful in life does not mean you have to change the world; it means meeting a need (regardless of the size) well and dependably over time and helping others overcome their pain and suffering from a tragic beginning.

My life has been transformed and changed for good by the power of my *beloved Creator*. This book will make you cry, laugh, and fill your soul with hope and inspiration to overcome this world and become the winner within.

Who says having a bad past can't create a great winner?

If I can do it, so can you!

These words were my lifeline and supported me through hard times, when I was drowning in pain and confusion.

It is my hope that you will find comfort in them as well.

Contents

My life was almost snuffed out,
The enemy was trying to kill, steal and destroy me!
Chaos and confusion became my greatest
companions, my innocence was taken from me, like
a Grim Reaper with an unsatisfiable desire.
Was it by chance my life was spared and saved?
"The thief comes only to steal and kill and destroy;
I have come that they may have life, and
have it to the full." (John 10:10)

It felt like I was in a prison cell—dark, damp, empty, and lonely from the silence and neglect I endured. No visitors, no food, no care, no love. Why did I exist? What was the point of having me?

Neglect is just as bad as being molested or raped, I came to find out later from experts in psychology. I was innocent. I didn't deserve such severe punishment, getting locked down to these walls that were closing in on me. I was a victim, yet convicted as a criminal until the prison door was unlocked and pushed wide open to set me free. I was scared and afraid to be free. I only knew what prison walls felt like, but deep within my soul, I knew there was a little girl within me that needed *help*. She needed to be set *free* and given a chance to become brave and strong. I needed to help her find the courage to take the first steps out of that hellish prison. There is only one who has a key to give freedom like this. I couldn't outperform my own belief systems. I had to learn a new way to burst out of the walls within my darkness and the limiting belief system in my mind. I needed a new belief system, and He came and gave me all that I needed and more.

Though my father and mother forsake me,

the LORD will receive me. (Psalm 27:10)

So do not fear, for I am with you;

do not be dismayed, for I am your God.

I will strengthen you and help you;

I will uphold you with my righteous right hand. (Isaiah 41:10)

In a desert land he found him,

in a barren and howling waste.

He shielded him and cared for him;

He guarded him as the apple of his eye. (Deuteronomy 32:10)

Introduction

I was lost and now I am found.

How wonderful to know that you're always wanted by your Creator who loves you and wants the best for you at all times, even from your beginning.

You were always wanted by *Him*.

We think we are born from our parents, but there is someone so much bigger and so much better than our parents, bigger than our grandparents, and bigger than anyone in this entire world. It's in the *unseen forces* of this world that you don't see—*a spiritual world*.

Even if you don't believe it, that doesn't mean it's not true or real.

The law of gravity is real; however, you don't see it. The law of electricity is real, but you don't need to understand it to use it.

Our world is governed by laws we do not need to see or even fully understand how to use. We don't need to know how they work.

You know that the law of gravity keeps you from floating into space, and the law of electricity allows you to light up a dark room.

Whether you're a good or a bad person, these laws still hold true.

The laws that govern this world do not discriminate. They don't care whether you're old or young, skinny or fat, rich or poor, what religious background, color, or race you belong to; it applies to *all*.

Another thing that is true for all is that *we all need a savior*!

No one is perfect, but we are all given one hundred percent potential by God, and it is our job to use that potential for man's greater good.

I became a hundred-watt bulb for my Creator.

I had to give up my old identity in order to be renewed through him. By allowing the love of God to restore my worth and self-love, I was able to go from feeling like a worthless, dirty, hopeless, shameful, broken young girl, robbed of her innocence and stuck in a place of complete dysfunction, to a woman of certainty, security, confidence, and love, fully restored and forgiven through the mighty love of her savior, forever valued and treasured.

The more you change your mental state of programming, the quicker your life will change for good.

"I have told you these things, so that in Me you may have peace. In this world you will have trouble. But take heart! *I have overcome the world*" (John 16:33).

It is an interesting fact of Jesus's teachings—and one that's often overlooked in our modern world—that both the followers of Christ and non-followers will go through suffering. No one is exempt. However, we are promised a life of abundance through Him, and through suffering, you will realize and understand that it produces great strength and power to overcome life's greatest adversities. These build greater character if you allow your pain to turn into triumph. That's why I'm writing this story, for you to see that you have a choice—to believe or not to believe. However, you have nothing to lose if you believe, but everything to gain.

He replied, "Because you have so little faith. Truly I tell you, if you have faith as small as a mustard seed, you can say to this mountain, 'Move from here to there,' and it will move. Nothing will be impossible for you" (Matthew 17:20).

You see, all you need is just a little faith. Faith is the assurance of things hoped for and the evidence of the things not seen. *Just believe* that there is a God who is for you and not against you. His ways are not our ways; His ways are higher than our ways, just as the heavens are higher than the earth.

Though called "the God of all comfort," He was known as "a man of many sorrows" and had great compassion for His people. Now He can identify with all mankind. He became flesh and blood for our sake.

What incredible love for those who need and want His magnificent love. Just saying, people in this world definitely don't have this magnificent love to give—that's for sure!

"Neither height nor depth, nor anything else in all creation, will be able to separate us from the Love of God" (Romans 8:39).

This world is steeped in deception and saturated with evil. How do we stay filled with greatness inside of us and be healthy and whole as an individual in such a world?

Because you can't give what you don't have!

You have to get it from someone who has it, so who has it?

What are we all looking for?

We all are desperately looking for unconditional love, and only God has it as He showed it through His one and only Son.

We all want someone to just burst inside our hearts and minds to open them up and fill them up to the brim, so that we can overflow into all those around us.

There is one who I know for sure can do such a thing. He did all of this for me, and He can do it for you as well—our Creator!

He created you and me inside our mothers' wombs before the beginning of time, and He goes and prepares a place for you and me in eternity. Now that's hope!

Pain and trials, however, are not limited; they come to all who find themselves in this strange world. The suffering and evil that afflicts us all is the result of mankind's capacity to choose evil over good, God's desire to allow us the ability to choose, for only a world with free will "makes possible any love, goodness, or joy worth having." And yet, suffering also serves another purpose. It is God's megaphone to rouse a deaf world, a sign that somewhere mankind has erred. It's a resounding call to seek only that which can satisfy us—our Creator's magnificent love.

My story is one of suffering for many years as a product of my environment. This is not extraordinary in itself, as suffering is as commonplace as life itself. Rather, this is an account of He who "carries us all the days of our lives," who never stops seeking us, even when we have long past given up on ourselves. This is a story of abuse, neglect, hardship, and loneliness. But ultimately, it is the story of someone broken and brokenhearted, who, after many years of chaos, confusion, and rebellion, finally decided to give God a chance. A God that I was so unfamiliar with, it took me ten years to learn to truly trust and rest in His security and certainty of who He said he really was. The I Am and the Alpha and Omega, the first and the last, the beginning and the end, the ETERNAL ONE.

Through laying bare my experiences, I run the risk of opening up my soul to strangers. However, I believe this to be necessary in order to accurately express my story. In modern society, we go to great lengths to hide our suffering and our mistakes, seeking at all costs to conceal from public view that we may be unhappy or burdened, deathly afraid that someone may see through the veil of our idyllic existence (either online or in person). But the honest seeker of truth is not fooled by the mirage. We live in a world scourged by loneliness and isolation. In the words of Arthur Schopenhauer, famous philosopher of metaphysics, "There is no doubt that life is given us, not to be enjoyed, but to be overcome; to be got over."

I suffered before I knew Christ, and I suffered after I knew Him in a different way because now I had someone to carry my pain for me. But the latter is not comparable to the former, for now I am filled with the *magnificent love* that comes from God, a love that surpasses knowledge and a peace that transcends understanding. It is my hope that everyone who reads this story may learn from the mistakes that I have made. Above all, I pray that they may be encouraged and led to Him, who has taken up all my burdens and given me rest, for "His yoke is easy, and His burden is light," and He has given me life more abundantly.

After all my trials and mistakes, I can now attest to the fact that joy is not necessarily the absence of suffering; it is the presence of God. I will add to that: suffering is not something you lose, it's something you gain from because it produces change, forcing us out of our comfort zone, pushing us to go to higher levels.

Chapter 1

Childhood Is Not Supposed to Be Like This

Everyone has those first memories of childhood: dim rays of light in the early years of our foggy existence, short pictures where, for the first time, we seem to be aware that we are alive and taking part in the world. My earliest memory is of an empty room with sunlight streaming through a window. The picture is fuzzy, like some camera lens fading in and out of focus, and my brother sits near me, crying. What is more striking than the physical details is the awareness of what is not there, a deep feeling of emptiness and loneliness characteristic of my memories at the time. Above the physical reality, there is also a sense of fear and alarm, as if my brain had chosen just this moment to jolt awake and begin recording.

It was not until years later that I learned that this was the time my mother decided she'd had enough of caring for us and abandoned my brother and me in an empty house. After a few days, someone finally came to pick us up. I was four years old when this happened.

My mother came back after some time. Then, she made it a habit to come back and leave again, until the final time when she packed all her bags and left for good. While I was crying, my frail little body was clothed in red velvet pants and a cute button-down shirt, with pigtails in my hair. I tried to ask her why she was packing her bags. I don't recall what she replied, but I can only imagine. My heart hurt and my stomach was queasy, and I was shaking and crying with her. It's so crazy that little children might not know what's going on, but they can feel what's going on inside of them. A big, long white car pulled up. My mother started to carry all her bags out to the trunk of this car, and then that was it. She took off. I ran after that car, crying, the tears running down my face. "No, Mama, please don't go, please don't leave," I screamed. "I promise to be a good girl. Please come back. Please, Mama! Please!" She vanished and never came back. That memory stayed with me for a long time. To think your mother didn't love you enough to take you with her, or that she wouldn't come back to get you has a profoundly negative effect on the psyche and is the worst thing a child can experience. A child doesn't understand adult things; their perceptions are fragile and broken. A child shuts down after such pain as it's too hard to process when no one is there to help them understand. So they go with it alone and isolate deep within themselves.

Memories like these, featuring loss and abandonment, became far too common a theme of my early years. It would be reassuring to say that I found comfort in my father's home, but sadly this was not the case. I have one clear memory of him not many years after my mother left. I listened to his rage and anger, screaming, "Casey, I will kill you! I will get even with you," as loud crashes and bangs were happening. My brother and I were in fear and trembling as we lay in our little bunk beds behind the living room wall, scared to death of what was happening on the other side. My father had turned the dining room into our bedroom. It was all brown paneling on the walls, and you can just imagine it: not only was it dark and dirty, it was very loud. We could hear him loud and clear. I hate brown paneled walls to this day as they bring back all the dreadful memories. I jumped in my brother's bed and we held onto each other for comfort until morning. If I could describe what it felt like in my little pounding heart, it would be like being outside watching or hearing a tornado that you couldn't find any refuge from. That's what it was like all too often for my brother and me. We couldn't wait for the tornado to stop as morning appeared. When my brother and I rounded the corner in our small apartment, we saw my dad sitting in a chair without a shirt, head resting backward in the air, a tube tied around his arm. Protruding from his vein was a thin, clear needle. I remember that I screamed, thinking he was dead. I doubt that my feeble attempt to feed him Fritos had any effect, but after some hours, he eventually woke up.

Fyodor Dostoevsky's, a Russian novelist's, famous quote said: "You must know that there is nothing higher and stronger and more wholesome and good for life in the future than some good memory, especially a memory of childhood, of home. People talk to you a great deal about your education, but some good, sacred memory, preserved from childhood, is perhaps the best education. If a man carries many such memories with him into life, he is safe to the end of his days, and if one has only one good memory left in one's heart, even that may sometimes be the means of saving us."

All can attest to the reality of Dostoevsky's words, but the sad fact is that his maxim can work in reverse too. A life marred by many such memories has the potential to linger with us, springing alive just when we least expect them to, weighing us down with anxiety and sorrow followed by depression.

Memory is a tool, and people create their worlds with the tools they have directly at hand. Faulty tools produce faulty results, and repeated use of them can create a cycle of heartbreak and pain that extends back generations, to parents and grandparents, children, and siblings. In order to understand my story, one has to understand the family I came from, and the sad cycle that finally ended with God's help.

Chapter 2

Oh No, Another Kid!

My father, Pete, was born on December 9, 1951, a product of two people who fell into love and then out of love. Their marriage and whirlwind romance did not last long, and shortly after my father was born, his parents got divorced, beginning a series of events that later culminated in three separate wrecked families. Each of his parents remarried and had large families, and it soon became clear that he was not wanted by either set of stepparents. To make matters worse, his biological mother, Barbara, became an alcoholic, adding to his misery.

In John's first New Testament letter, he says, "We love because he first loved us." If only he had received the love God provides—how different his life could have been! Sadly, it would be years before he heard any good News, and those formative years irrevocably stunted his life. Pete could never really grasp what it meant to love someone else. Like some toy soldier, always playing the part but never becoming alive, my father stumbled through life, always failing to grasp what it meant to love my brother and me. For him, the old saying, "You can't give what you don't have" applied.

As my father entered adolescence, he continued to regress. Unloved, unwanted, and hated by Tina, his stepmother, he found a family with all the wrong people and took solace in drugs. Alcohol, rage, abuse, abandonment, isolation, and self-sabotage became staples of his life, and at the age of fifteen, he met my mom, Bonnie, who had a similar background to his own. Shortly after, she became pregnant and gave birth to a son on December 17, 1968, who they named Mark. Not long after his birth, my mother became pregnant again, and on February 3, 1970, I was born.

I can only imagine the fear and confusion that my mother must have experienced during the time she was pregnant with us. How scared she must have been at the tender age of sixteen, and how easily she could have listened to the voices in her life urging her toward abortion! In spite of all the blunders my mother made later on in life, I am forever grateful that she chose life. As David says in Psalm 139, "You created my inmost being; you knit me together in my mother's womb…your eyes saw my unformed body. All the days ordained for me were written in your book before one of them came to be."

Against all the odds, my mother decided to keep both me and my brother. It is comforting to realize that God was protecting me even in my mother's womb, for my story could have ended even before it began. Even in the midst of a hopeless situation, with two broken teenagers barely able to support themselves, God was working for my good. It was into this strange family that God placed me, and He has never abandoned me, even though at times I could not see Him there.

Chapter 3

Scared and Confused

Raising children is never easy. As every parent knows, bringing kids into the world is a balancing act that tests even the most well-prepared individuals. For the two scared teenagers who were my parents, it seemed from the start that the task they had been given was outside the scope of their ability. My mother fared the worst. Empty and depressed from the situation she found herself in, and often on the end of physical abuse received from my father, my mom finally decided she had had enough.

In the book of Isaiah, the Old Testament prophet compared God's great love for his people to that of a mother and her child. He wrote, "Can a mother forget her nursing child? Can she feel no love for the child she has borne? See, I have engraved you on the palms of my hands; your walls are ever before me" (Isaiah 49:15–16). For many years, I struggled to come to terms with my mother's disappearance. How was it possible that she left us when we needed her the most? Looking around at other kids and their mothers, I realized

I would never experience what they had, and I grew bitter in spirit. Much of my childhood was spent searching for a way to fill the void she had left in my life.

Although I eventually learned to forgive my mother, her departure only served to deepen my father's pain. The bitterness and rage that had been aimed at her was now directed at us, and in a short time, we began to experience the full force of his anger. Beatings occurred often. He would grab us, drag us to his room, hold us down, and whip us with his belt. As his drug and alcohol use intensified, smaller and more arbitrary offenses incurred his abuse. Spill a glass of milk and you were scared, just waiting for a blow to the back of the head, our screams rattling down the hallways of our shabby apartment. It became so common that our teeth would chatter in fear when my father came home from work, and we began to wonder if it would be better if he didn't come home at all. It's so strange to look back as a little girl and understand what was really happening, but it doesn't matter. You don't know what you don't know. Your perception becomes so distorted. It can take years of therapy to understand and just to be okay, so that you can change the way you perceive those things. Had I known what I know now, I could have saved myself years of pain and trauma.

On one occasion, I was playing with the phone in our apartment when I accidentally pulled a little cord out of the bottom. Frozen with panic, I hung it up and retreated to my room, not mentioning to anyone what had happened. I lay on my bed for hours, a deep knot in my stomach as I waited for the door to open, marking my father's return. Finally, I heard the sound of his entrance and the expected string of shouts and curses as he realized his connection with his drug dealers had been cut off. I still remember his snarling face as he confronted me, his eyes bulging out of his head. In my terror, I thought of the only way out—I blamed my brother. Barging into his room, my father gave Mark the beating of his life at my expense. I carried the guilt of my lie for years, another event that led me to blame myself for my miserable existence.

My brother and I weren't the only ones on the end of my father's beatings. As we grew older, a string of women would come to live in our little apartment, some for a few days and some for years. Although they were of all ages and backgrounds, each of them departed in the same manner: bruised and broken. Nothing in my life has made me feel more helpless than the crying, piercing screams of my father's girlfriends throughout the night. I remember on multiple occasions thinking that someone was being murdered. My brother and I wanted to rescue them, but we were always rooted in place, mustering only the energy to shake and cry. Inevitably, the same phrases came echoing through the door: "Where did you put my pills? I'm going to kill you if you don't tell me where they are."

Oddly enough, the worst part of the ordeal was watching each girlfriend move their furnishings out the next morning. All I saw was a potential mom leaving. I always had great hopes for each of the women that visited us, believing against all evidence that this one would stay long enough to love and cherish me. Although each girl-friend left, the nightmares of their screams remained, lingering with me long after I had grown up.

Chapter 4

Being Held Hostage

When I was around six years old, my father's addiction to drugs seemed to take an ever-increasing role in his life, and his attitude toward us grew strange and aloof. As for so many of those who struggle with substance abuse, reality became an inconvenience that came to be ignored. My dad began to disappear for long periods of time, and my brother and I were often left to fend for ourselves. Sitting alone in our dilapidated apartment became the chief way for us to spend our time.

One night stands out above all the others. After coming home late from work, our father announced that he wanted to take us to see a movie. My brother and I were more than a little shocked, but also secretly thrilled at the unexpected night out. We were giddy as we drove to the theater, and in our excitement, we even let out a few laughs in the back seat. But what we saw in the theater that night left us scarred. My dad had taken us to see *The Exorcist*, and it left a permanent imprint on my mind.

What we choose to put into our minds can have a profound impact on the way we think and act. At the age of six, I began to experience insomnia, with the demonic nature of the movie leaving me unable to sleep soundly for years afterward. I came to believe that the devil was trying to kill, steal, and destroy me. I thought he lived under our bunk beds, and that his hand would reach out of the toilet bowl to suck me in.

To make matters worse, I began to have recurring nightmares that would wake me up at night in tears, further aggravating my father's temper.

How often children are hostage to their parents' dysfunction, and how I wanted someone to rescue us and to heal all my wounds! I longed for someone to speak to about my pain and my neglect, but there was no one in my life to whom I could turn. One night I lay crying on my father's bed when he came home drunk. Lying down next to me on the bed, he tried to touch me in the wrong spot. Immediately, I knew something wasn't right. I ran out of the room into the bathroom and stayed there until my father passed out. My father remembered the incident the next morning and was deeply hurt at what he had done. But the event only served as a further testament to the drug-fueled degeneracy that had engulfed his life.

Chapter 5

The Enemy

I wish I could say that I never again had to endure sexual abuse from those who watched over me, but I would not escape so easily. Just as grime and filth attract roaches, so does the neglect and isolation in which my brother and I lived drew monsters that would come to terrorize my life. It started when some of our extended family moved into our apartment complex. Everyone liked my Uncle Buddy. He was handsome, charming, and smooth, as well as a recognized radio jockey who was a hero to many people. Unfortunately, he was also a pedophile.

The abuse began when I was five. My father would often ask Buddy to look after my brother and me when he left for extended periods, resulting in a sadly predictable situation where my uncle had access to us for hours on end. He would lure me into the bathroom, saying, "You show me yours, and I'll show you mine." Touching me and stimulating me, he would do things that cannot be named, for "it is shameful even to mention what the disobedient do in secret"

(Ephesians 5:12). As with all predators, Buddy identified and exploited the obvious hole in my life—a desperate need for love and affection. At times it felt good to be loved, but it was so wrong, so confusing, so sad.

The exploitation wasn't limited to my waking hours. In our apartment in East Brunswick, there was a big glass sliding door in the back room where my brother and I slept in our bunk beds. I used to beg my brother to let me sleep on the top bunk so that my uncle couldn't pull me out of the bed to take me to the bathroom. Until I was eleven years old, I would lie awake at night, staring at the brown paneling on the walls, dreading that I would hear the sound of those doors open.

In spite of the hopeless situation I found myself in, there always seemed to be some kind of presence that I felt near me, an unseen force watching over me. I would cry and talk to these unseen forces. It is doubtful I could have survived those years without it. At the time I didn't know exactly what it was, but I thought that it might be God Himself or an angel that God sent to care for me. It is only with hindsight that I can say that even as a young girl, God had begun to reveal Himself to me.

How impossible it is for God to forget those little ones who "always see the face of their father in heaven" (Matthew 18:10). Although I was five years old and always dirty, and there was no one to give us a bath, to do our laundry, or to feed us, I now know that my Heavenly Father had never abandoned me for a single day. And it was through His will that He eventually placed someone in our life who would begin to alleviate some of our burdens.

Chapter 6

Finally, Some Refuge

It began in the usual way, with an unknown woman sleeping over at our apartment for a night. The situation had occurred countless times before, and my brother and I expected very little from it. But as nights turned to days, and days to weeks, I started to grow anxious. Something strange was happening; the woman who had come was not leaving, and it even looked like she was moving her stuff in! I came to find out that the woman's name was Sharon, and her stay became a blessed relief from the drudgery of our existence.

Sharon was a keeper. I never wanted to let her go. She stayed for about four or five years. I still remember asking her if I could call her mom, a question I put to all of my father's girlfriends. I was so desperate to be loved. When she enthusiastically said yes, I knew that I had found someone who was truly different. She was a special one that really gave us time and attention, and she took us with her to her parents' house often. I still remember them to this day. They were also great people. Sharon was kind to my brother and me, always making sure we were clean and well-fed. She often bought us clothes and would allow our friends over to play with us, lessening some of our loneliness. She even found time to take us to church, planting the seed of God's great love.

Looking back at my early childhood, I am reminded of Shakespeare's quote on kindness: "How far that little candle throws its beams! So shines a good deed in a weary world." Sharon certainly proved to be a God-sent light in my life. Although Buddy's visits never stopped, for the first time I began to understand what it meant to love and be loved. Her time with us ushered in a period of stability in what seemed like a tumultuous situation. Sharon didn't always have it easy though. Like so many others, she found herself on the end of my father's physical abuse, and though she was able to control him for years, his drug addiction overtook him once again.

As my father lost control, his violence grew worse. Amazingly, Sharon was able to weather the storm, but she was always fighting a losing battle. One night, the situation came to a head. In an explosion of rage, he hurt Sharon and the police were called in. The evidence was undeniable; my father was completely lost. He needed a major change in his life if he ever wanted to resume a normal existence. He finally chose to go into a rehabilitation facility in Newark for two years. In the end, it proved to be an easy decision. Although rehab would completely separate him from Mark and me, it was better for all of us in the long run.

Although God has never rescinded his command to honor our father and mother, he did tell fathers "not to embitter their children."

When I turned ten, I was now old enough to realize the extent of my father's delinquency, and his sudden exit from my life filled me with a simmering rage that would not be extinguished until I laid it at the cross of Christ years later. To forgive my father at this time would have been impossible; I had neither the love nor the desire to over-look someone who had hurt me so many times, and this resentment spilled out into other parts of my life.

When Sharon took us in following my father's departure, I began to rebel. Lies, deception, bitterness, and anxiety gained a foothold in my life, and though she loved me and Mark, our behavior proved too much for her to handle. After one year of taking care of us, poor finances and the burden of raising two kids led her to decide to pass us off to our grandparents. On a cold, windy autumn day in 1980, Sharon exited our lives. I do not remember much of her departure, except that I believed I would never see her again. It was a crushing blow. Once more, my world had been turned upside down, and the same questions began to swirl in my mind. Did I have something to do with all the people who abandoned me? Was it all my fault?

Chapter 7

Shaky Ground

Sharon's sudden departure meant that for the time being, we were in the hands of Child Protective Services, and they gave us a choice: move in with Buddy or live with my grandparents. How thankful I am that God put it in the hearts of those in charge of us to let us decide! At ten years old, I explained that I wanted to stay with my grandparents, even though we had not had much contact with them in the past. So at the end of the year, Mark and I found ourselves standing at the door of my Grandpa Hank's house. He lived with his wife, Tina, who despised my father.

Any illusions we had about our new home were quickly dispelled upon our arrival. After entering, Tina led us to a small, dark room in the back of the cellar where a rickety bunk bed stood against the wall. We were told that this was our new "room," the place we would spend every night. As I lay crying on the top bunk that first night, I could have echoed Jonah's lament as he found himself in the belly of the fish: "You hurled me into the depths, into the very heart of the seas, and the currents swirled about me; all your waves and breakers swept over me." Despite the rough start, I earnestly believed things would get better. However, as so often happened in those early years of my life, reality seemed to find a way to crush my spirit and expectations.

As soon as we settled in, it became evident that my brother and I were not wanted there. We were not allowed to go upstairs much, nor were we permitted to go into the fridge or cabinets when we were hungry. What, where, and when we ate was decided by Tina, who ran the house with an iron fist that relegated my grandfather to the role of a passive observer. Despite his weak-willed protests, Tina never failed to remind us that we existed as a consequence of their good graces and that we were, at best, nothing more than a burden. She was often fond of saying that I "would be the death of my grandfather" because he loved us and took more than a passing interest in our welfare. As our stay went on, Tina's negativity and bullying began to take a toll on my mental health. In a sad twist of fate, it seemed that the hatred she had for my father so many years before had been rekindled, with its outpouring now directed at us.

Ironically, the loveless situation Mark and I found ourselves in could have been avoided if my grandfather had only spoken up. He truly loved us but was always afraid to show it. The renowned psychologist Jordan Peterson is noted as saying, "If you think tough men are dangerous, wait until you see what weak men are capable of." Though my grandfather could have stepped in at any moment, he allowed the emotional abuse to continue.

Shaky Ground

Despite his shortcomings, my grandfather's poem about me is a testament to the love he had hidden deep inside for us:

KIM...THERE IS NOT A GIFT WORTH OF YOU... in all this world
SO ALL I CAN GIVE YOU IS MY HEART...

OH NO ANOTHER BABY WE COULD HARDLY FEED THE FIRST
HOPES WERE DIM MOM & DAD WERE JUNKIES TIMING WAS AT ITS WORST
SURE SHE WAS SO VERY CUTE EVERYONE WOULD ADMIT
BUT WE WERE ALL SUFFERING DRUGS, ABOUT AS BAD AS IT COULD GET
DAD WAS SO THIN, AN ERIE PASTY WHITE, & MOM HAD RUN AWAY
THE CHILDREN MOVED AROUND, WONDERING WHERE THE NIGHT WOULD STAY
THIS WAS THE FIRE THAT WOULD FORGE THEIR FUTURE STANCE...
THIS IS THE CHARACTER, THIS LONG BRUTAL TEST WOULD ENHANCE
GOOD OR BAD AS IF BY CHOICE OR RANDOM CHANCE
GODS SUNSHINE WOULD LITE THE WAY TO BETTER YEARS
& STILL THEIR POUNDING HEAR S & QUELL THEIR BITTER FEARS
& MOLD & TEMPER FROM A GASTLY BLEAK & PAINFUL PAST
THE TRUE & UNSELFISH CHARACTER THAT WOULD FOREVER LAST
THE GIRL CHILD, LIKE A GOOD SHEPARD, BRING MANY TO THE FOLD
& SHINE IN HIS, & EVERYONES EYES AS PURE & PRICELESS GOLD...

grampy...

A treasured photo of Mark and me when my
dad, Pete, tried to show us love

Many of my nights were spent crying myself to sleep, wondering if there was anyone in the world who truly wanted me or loved me. Although I didn't know it at the time, I began to experience symptoms of depression, such as a lack of will to live and the constant urge to kill myself. The months of bullying had also damaged my self-worth, and I felt as if I had no value. If only I had known how much worth I had in God's sight—that there was a great God who loved and valued me and deemed me as important! Despite my lack of knowledge, my God provided relief for me in other ways.

My grandpa Hank and I

Chapter 8

Some Sort of Stability

Throughout my life, school had always served as a refuge for me, a safe place where I could escape from the tumult of my time at home. But that changed when we moved in with our grandparents. As a result of leaving East Brunswick, I was forced to start fifth grade in a different school, a difficult task at any age. Two of the first students I met were Karen and Jodi. One night, we were invited to a movie by the same mutual friends, who were grounded at the last second. Karen and I still went, even though we didn't like one another. But that began a lifelong friendship as best friends. Her friendship provided a valuable outlet from my grandparents and helped me to weather the storms that I went through at home.

As I got to know Karen better, I found that we had so many common bonds, and though Karen's mother was in her life, she was not mentally stable. Though we came from greatly dysfunctional families and relationships, our experiences only brought us closer together. We felt like two rebels fighting a hard battle against a crazy world. As in so many friendships, banding together with friends always involves a bit of defiance against the rest of society.

My grandmother, however, continued to make our lives at home miserable. One day, she punished me for leaving a board game on the back porch. I do not remember whether I was inspired by my newfound confidence, or whether I'd simply had enough, but I made the decision to run away. After walking miles to my Grandma Helen's (my mother's mother's) house, I called Karen and her mother and asked them to pick me up. It seemed that the incident affected my grandparents because my grandfather finally stood up to Tina. When I returned home, her attitude toward me was pacified, and my Grandpa Hank even bought me a bike.

Although there was never much love at my grandparents' house, I learned that there are always people in our lives we can be grateful for. Though Karen was my best friend, I also came to rely on my brother. At that time, we didn't fight much but tried to help each other as best we could. Today, I am frequently reminded of the words of Elisabeth Elliot, who said, "It is always possible to be thankful for what is given rather than to complain about what is not given. One or the other becomes a habit of life."

Chapter 9

Longing for a Mom

It was during the end of this period that memories of my mother began to resurface, and I started to think deeply about what she was like and where she had gone. My journals in this period reflect the sense of loss that I felt when I thought about her. In one poem, I wrote:

My world had fallen apart, because
The mother I really wanted was
Stolen from my little heart.
You never called. I hid behind the tears
And my great big smile.

Maybe it was the sense of heartache I felt in this period that put the idea into my head. Whatever the reason, I soon recruited Karen in an effort to find my birth mom. We reached out to my grandmother Helen, who I had heard had contacted my mom from time to time. When she saw that we were serious, she promised to do all she could to locate my mother. Weeks passed, and we heard nothing. Just when I prepared myself for the possibility that I would never see her, we received a call from my grandmother. Amazingly, my mom had turned up as a patient in a hospital in South Amboy, just a fifteen-minute drive away from where we lived. So on a warm spring day, Karen and I took the long walk to the hospital to see my mother. It took us a couple of hours to get there, and we arrived tired and worn out.

It would be impossible to describe my emotional state as we strode past the front desk. I felt scared, happy, sad, and angry all at once. At eleven years old, it seemed as if I were reaching into the past to view some figure I had long since thought dead. I had no idea what to say, or what to call her. When I entered the room, all I could muster were the words, "Hi, Bonnie!"

Although I had dreamed of many fantastic scenarios for our meeting, there was one I had not thought of—the ordinary and the mundane. Bonnie greeted me with a hug and kiss, then went on to act as if we had seen each other last week. She offered no tears at our greeting, no shock at seeing my face, and no apology for leaving me. We casually swapped phone numbers, and she promised to call me. She never did. I left feeling more confused and rejected than ever, certain that I had missed some crucial detail that would shed light on the whole encounter. But the reality slowly dawned on me; Bonnie had no interest in my life. Our meeting was nothing more than an item on her to-do list, an uncomfortable fact that she had to entertain in order to go on with her day.

Chapter 10

Lost

My remaining months at my grandparents' house were long and arduous, and my despair at failing to reconnect with my mother only added to my pain. Without the help of my brother Mark and Karen, I'm not sure I would have made it through. But just when there seemed to be no end in sight, a ray of light dawned in our dark cellar. We learned that my dad, Pete, had been released from rehab after two years and that we were going to live with him. I was overjoyed. To add to my delight, my father appeared to have changed since I last saw him. He had completely kicked his drug addiction and even began to spend some quality time with us. It felt like I was dreaming. It seemed that in the space of a few weeks, God had taken us out of darkness and into His wonderful light. It is always helpful to remember that our trials do not last forever. As the apostle Peter said, "The God of all grace, who called you to his eternal glory in Christ, after you have suffered a little while, will himself restore you and make you strong, firm and steadfast" (1 Peter 5:10).

Pete's transformation ushered in a period of normalcy that Mark and I had not experienced in the past. Without drugs, our father remained free to care for us as he always intended to, and our home life felt stable and secure. But as the weeks progressed, cracks began to show in my father's extraordinary character change. For one, many more women would come over and spend the night with him, leading to a continual sequence of new faces that departed as quickly as they came. Although my father had conquered his drug addiction, it seemed that he had only substituted one vice for another. His mental ills had been cured, but spiritually, he remained as childlike as ever.

Sadly, my father's behavior in these years set an example that I would follow through my adolescence. Despite Pete's sexual deviancy, I came to respect him and look up to him. This was due to the natural adoration all children have for their parents, but also because I had no other examples in my life. As a young girl, I wrote in my journal, "He is my inspiration for what I want in a man. I love him and admire him more than anyone else can imagine."

I soon began to follow in my father's footsteps. When I was twelve years old, I started smoking, and at the age of thirteen, I started drinking too. I was always an outgoing girl after busting out of that inner prison that kept me locked up for way too long, and it was time to grow and make friends. However, my newfound independence led me to embrace the lifestyle I had seen played out in my home so many times before. It was made all the easier by Karen's parents' lack of supervision; they wanted to be our friends, which allowed us to party at her house as much as we pleased. Although I always feared drugs because of the disastrous effects I had seen as a child, I never felt as if alcohol was off-limits. In time, binge drinking would become a normal part of my routine and a source of much grief and pain as I got older.

Chapter 11

Dysfunction Repeating Itself

As is so often the case in life, one sin opens the door to many others.

Fueled by the partying and drinking that now dominated my social scene, I began to date guys and sleep around. My lifestyle was only exacerbated by my emotional state. Although I was often the life of the party, inwardly, I was hounded by insecurity, worthlessness, and a longing for love. At the age of thirteen, I began to seek out boys to satisfy the emptiness I felt inside, hoping that their attention would make me feel worthy. It was at this age that I developed a problem that went on to plague me throughout my life—the inability to determine if a boy really loved me. The truth is, I had no examples to emulate except the one that was played out in my father's bedroom night after night. I believed that if a boy stayed with me for a month or two and I slept with him, that meant he loved me. Of course, my pain after these trysts only intensified, for as Augustine says, "You have made us for Yourself, O Lord, and our heart is restless until it rests in You."

In his love letter to his expected bride, the biblical King Solomon wisely states, "Daughters of Jerusalem, I charge you: Do not arouse or awaken love until it so desires" (Song of Solomon 8:4). The truth is that sex is so much more than a meaningless physical action. Although our culture relegates sexual intercourse to a casual relationship with few lasting implications, sex involves a level of intimacy not experienced in any other human relationship. When God brought Adam and Eve together in marriage, he tells us that a man will leave his family, join his wife, and become "one flesh" (Genesis 2:24).

Instead of bringing greater fulfillment, my lifestyle of free love only served to deepen the hole in my life. When we seek to fill a void with feelings and emotions, we will never find contentment. The void can only be filled through the spiritual consciousness that comes from knowing God.

It wasn't long before the consequences of my lifestyle caught up with me. When I was fifteen years old, I learned that I was pregnant. This news shocked and terrified me. The same series of events that had ruined the lives of both my parents was now repeating itself; such is the lot of all those who turn their backs to God. As it is written, "I, the LORD your God, am a jealous God, punishing the children for the sin of the parents to the third and fourth generation of those who hate me, but showing love to a thousand generations of those who love me and keep my commandments" (Exodus 20:5–6). God is just, and the cycles of degeneracy that engulfed my family in these years were undoubtedly the punishment of one who sought to turn us from the error of our ways. At this time, however, there seemed to be no end in sight to the immorality that plagued my family for generations.

The realization that I was pregnant led me to turn to my father for guidance, and he instructed me to abort the baby. I complied and took "the pill." I had few qualms at the time when I flushed out my system; I thought of it only as a procedure on my bladder that was preferable to the pain of an operation. It was only after I had committed the act that I was hit with the full recognition of what I had done. I began to be haunted by a guilt that would not be driven out, and it ate away at me until it threatened to consume me. I thought of what my child would have looked like and how old he would be, and the pain of encountering other children was often too intense to bear. At certain times, I wanted to kill myself. I was tormented until I started to believe in Him who forgives all our sins and transgressions and makes us pure and white as snow. However, that day was still years away.

Chapter 12

Trying to Fill the Void

Robert Frost once said, "In three words I can sum up everything I've learned about life: It goes on." Time has no choice but to move forward, and I soon found myself entering my junior year of high school, albeit with a new burden added to my existing load of trauma. I was soon caught up in the parties and drama that dominate high school, and there was always alcohol to block out my pain. It was here that I first met a boy named Pete (ironically with the same name as my dad) who I would go on to date on and off for ten years. Although we first got to know each other as juniors, it wasn't until the following summer that I took an interest in him.

Pete had a good childhood. He had a stable family that stuck together through thick and thin and a mom and dad who loved him very much and stayed married his whole life. I was so attracted to him, and of course, since my dad was super handsome, I went after guys who were super good-looking. However, I was always trying to find someone to fix and fill the void in my life. We were both trying to fill a void. Our relationship always teetered on the verge of collapse, a love affair between two people who were lost and broken.

From the start, our relationship was wracked with instability and distrust. Although we had genuine moments of love, Pete often cheated on me with various women, leaving me ashamed and bitter. Although Christ instructs us not to take revenge, but "to leave room for God's wrath," I retaliated by cheating on him instead of forgiving him and moving on. I was spiteful, wicked, and vicious. I would curse him out, yelling and screaming at him for looking at other girls. Insecurity dominated my character, and it was obvious to anyone I encountered.

It seemed that we broke up a hundred times, yet always found some way back to each other. And in spite of all our turmoil, after three years, we decided to move in together. How naive we were, and how comfortable we were living in dysfunction! No amount of ignorance, however, could blind me to the fact that Pete was not fully committed. Though I attempted to overlook the obvious, Pete often spent weekends drinking, and some nights he wouldn't come home at all. A few times, different women even called our phone explaining that he was fooling around and cheating on me, a source of much grief and pain.

Despite my knowledge of Pete's character, I still lacked the power to leave him. Drinking had now become the chief way Pete and I spent our time together, and we lived purely for the weekend. I became extremely codependent. Fearful to leave, I was constantly in fight or flight mode. Fights now consumed all of our waking hours, and we had little respect for each other. Our relationship, like our alcohol consumption, was now only a habit that we could not tear ourselves away from. Although it made our lives miserable, it also provided a false sense of security we had not experienced in any other aspect of our lives. It was like party time—you think that maybe you can find some joy for a few hours, but it always left me more depleted than I was before. The most dangerous thing I did was to believe in Pete's lies, which hurt me as much as believing my own lies and deception, thinking this was going to get better. It's easier to live in a fantasy world than face the truth that can set you free. God's word says the truth shall set you free.

Chapter 13

Having No Clue What Love Is

Without love, every relationship is doomed to fail. As I turned twenty-one, my dysfunctional relationship began to get increasingly worse, and I began to suffer emotional abuse. One night at a local club, a drunken spat between me and Pete ended with him shoving me down to the ground in the middle of the party. I was only saved from further blows by the quick-thinking bouncers who restrained him. It finally became clear to me that I needed to make a change in my life, and in November 1991, I finally decided to leave for good. Yet even as I was moving my things out, I was torn. I conceded in my journal that "if Pete did call me, I would probably break down and give in."

Though I knew deep down what was right, I could not bring myself to do it. My darkness was crouching at the door. I was only a slave to bondage and dysfunction, and the fleshly nature that lived in me was more powerful than my will to break away from my degenerative lifestyle. Though I knew Pete did not know how to meet the needs of a broken, wounded girl, or how to respect me, I had no power to escape from the comfort and familiarity of our relationship, and I hated myself for it. I lacked such value in myself. The shift came when I finally began to value myself. Because the measure you measure yourself with, others will perceive you at.

Although I had returned to a dysfunctional relationship, Jesus says, "Where your treasure is, there your heart will be also." For the thousandth time, I had placed my heart in the things of this world, and they had failed me yet again. I was utterly broken. I had no confidence and trust left in myself and no belief that I could do anything good or that I was worthy enough of healthy, good love. You don't know what you haven't learned. Time after time, I had failed to break free from the degenerative habits that characterized my lifestyle, and I hated what I had become. My life was marked by darkness and regret: "sexual immorality, impurity, debauchery, hatred, jealousy, fits of rage, selfish ambition, envy, and drunkenness." The burdens I had been carrying for years were crushing me, and I could go no further. Monkey see, monkey do. The apple doesn't fall far from the tree. I was inadvertently following in my father's footsteps.

In the Sermon on the Mount, my Creator charts the course of a believer's spiritual journey in the Beatitudes, a series of eight short sentences that demonstrate the inward life of a child of God. In the first verse, Jesus sets the foundation toward a shift in the heart. He states, "Blessed are the poor in spirit, for theirs is the kingdom of heaven."

The poor in spirit are those who are not rich in the eyes of the world. They do not have many material possessions, great wealth, or any pride in their own abilities. The relentless waves and turmoil of life have hollowed them out, and they are able to glimpse the hopelessness of their state. It is these people that Jesus speaks of in the next verse. "Blessed are those who mourn, for they will be comforted." Their peculiar nature has produced in them a state of longing which cannot be satisfied by anything in the world. They grieve over their condition, and in time, receive the comfort that God can provide. "People want their circumstances to change but they're unwilling to change themselves," says John Maxwell.

Little did I know that at the lowest point of my life, I had moved within reach of God's magnificent love. The failures and sufferings I had endured had made me ripe for God's unconditional love and forgiveness, and it was not long before Jesus placed someone in my path who would show me the truth. The Good Shepherd had almost finished his pursuit of me, and like some weary soldier swaying from innumerable wounds, the moment had arrived when I would cease my unbelief and rebellion and lay down my sword.

Chapter 14

Confusion at Its Finest

If I want to be free,

then I need to be me

and not the me that you think that I should be.

If I want to be free,

then I need to be me

and not the me that my friends want me to be.

If I want to be free,

then I need to be me

and not the me that my husband or wife wants me to be.

If I want to be free,

then I need to be me

and I need to find who me is.

(I love these beautifully true lines that

I heard at a seminar by Bob Proctor.)

As He patiently waited for the moment when I gave my heart to embrace My Redeemer, in December of 1991, that moment arrived for me. At twenty-one years old, I worked as a stylist at Inner Vision, a salon on Ernston Road in Sayreville, New Jersey. Though I smiled and worked with enthusiasm, I held in tears that threatened to burst forth at any moment. It was here that I met a woman named Irene. She was one of my clients and a mystery to me. Day after day, she would speak to me about Jesus. I thought she was a little crazy, but I liked to listen to her. There was something about her words that drew me in, though I could not name what it was. I felt as Herod must have felt when he sat listening to John the Baptist, for "Herod feared John and protected him, knowing him to be a righteous and holy man. When Herod heard John, he was greatly puzzled; yet he liked to listen to him" (Mark 6:20).

I didn't understand all of what Irene was telling me; still, her words gave me such comfort. I sensed a kind of inner peace that I had not yet experienced. One day, Irene shared the news that she had lost her unborn baby after five months, yet she was neither angry nor shattered. She maintained that there was a greater plan for her life than one she could see. I was amazed, and when Irene told me to go to a certain church in the area, I toyed with the idea. My mind started to fill with doubts. *What does church have to do with anything?* I thought to myself, *How could that help me?* I still saw the world only as purely physical. I did not understand that we are spirit as well as flesh: MIND-BODY-SPIRIT. You can't see the mind or the spirit, but you have evidence of the body. I realize more now than ever before that the unseen world is more real and has more power than the things you can see.

For some time, I fought with the idea of going to church, my mind wavering between two opinions like a wave tossed to-and-fro by the sea. After three months, I finally gave in, and on a cold December day in 1991, I made my way to church. I didn't like it. It was so different from anything I had ever experienced, and I felt like an outsider at a secret meeting I wasn't invited to. But as I left, I received a free Bible, which seemed to make the visit worthwhile. When I got home, I opened it and began to read. I only intended to skim through certain passages, but as I looked at the page, a verse caught my eye. It said, "Do not hide your face from me, do not turn your servant away in anger; you have been my helper. Do not reject me or forsake me, O God my Savior. Though my father and mother forsake me, the LORD will receive me" (Psalm 27:9–10). I had to imprint these life verses to my subconscious mind. I couldn't believe this could be true.

I was moved, and I read further. I encountered another verse that said, "For You formed my inmost being; you knit me together in my mother's womb. I praise You, for I am fearfully and wonderfully made; your works are wonderful, I know that full well. My frame was not hidden from You when I was made in the secret place, when I was woven together in the depths of the earth. Your eyes saw my unformed body; all my days ordained for me were written in your book before one of them came to be" (Psalm 139:13–16).

After this one, I was in awe. Why would a God say I was wonderful and marvelous? Does He have any idea how bad I am and all the wrong and bad things I have done?

A reading session I had intended to last a few minutes turned into two weeks, and in that time, the Lord opened my mind to understand His Word. I was overwhelmed by the love I found in the Bible, and I wanted to know and understand that love. "Taste and see that the Lord is good," says David in the Psalms. "Blessed is the man who trusts in Him!" (Psalm 34:8)

I decided to give God a chance; it was a love I had been searching for my whole life. I had nothing to lose, and everything to gain. So at twenty-one years old, I gave my life to my Creator and believed in the name of God's one and only Son.

Chapter 15

My Rescuer

The effects of my decision were instantaneous. It seemed that without even noticing a change, I felt loved and an inner peace for the first time in my life. I was filled with a "love that surpasses knowledge" and a "peace that transcends understanding." No longer did I feel worthless or unloved, for I knew that the Creator of the universe loved me unconditionally. I was overjoyed. I became kind, compassionate, caring, and a lover of people. The more I trusted God, the more my life got better and better.

The burdens that had consumed me for so long were lightened, for I was no longer so concerned about myself. Though I still felt that nothing good lived in me, I knew that didn't matter, because I now possessed God himself, living in me—a prize worth more than all the riches of the earth. As CS Lewis writes, "He who has God and everything else has no more than he who has God only." It seemed that the curse of Adam, the curse of my family, and the curse of my upbringing had all been undone in an instant. Now I didn't want to be mean, spiteful, or jealous any longer. I didn't even have the desire to drink anymore.

My heart burned within me to read God's Word every day. It felt like a love letter addressed to me and I couldn't get enough of His words, it felt as if it was God's personal diary. I sensed that I had a lot to learn, and He had a lot to teach. I became a woman of faith and hope, and I surrendered most of me—except the one part I wanted to keep at a distance, and that was my boyfriend, Pete. Despite the dysfunction, I still loved him, and I chose to put him first in my life. With smooth talk and flattery, Pete promised he would change, and I believed him. I was still an infant in learning God's ways, and I began to compromise.

But God's work does not end because a soul has crossed over from death to life. On the contrary, it is only the beginning. A new life conversion does not mean they have been purged of the human nature they have inherited from their ancestors. It only means that they have been given a new spirit, which, for the rest of my life, battles against my human nature.

I could relate to Paul, the apostle, who describes the conflict in this way: "So I find this law at work: Although I want to do good, evil is right there with me. For in my inner being I delight in God's law; but I see another law at work in me, waging war against the law of my mind and making me a prisoner of the law."

He states that it is only through the Holy Spirit that a believer can overcome the darkness that still exists in their life because the

"Lord is the Spirit, and where the Spirit of the Lord is, there is freedom." Now I had to make a conscious decision to choose to walk according to the Spirit or the flesh.

For the first time in my life, I now had a choice. It wasn't easy. I was always in conflict until I really learned that I could trust God one hundred percent. It was always His kindness that would lead me to repentance. God just has this way about Him to burst into my heart and fill it up with His words of love and kindness, affirming that I was truly His precious baby girl.

I couldn't understand how such a great God could really love me that way. All the things that used to make me happy, so I thought, actually left me emptier. It was my perception that really started to change, but it took me time to let go of old bad habits that I was so deeply entrenched in. I could choose between my old way of life and thinking, or the new way. The new way would prove challenging, and in my weakness, I often stumbled back into the old convenient and comfortable habits. God says, for what does righteousness and wickedness have in common? Or what fellowship can light have with darkness?

Pete's behavior seemed to justify my fears. He remarked that he didn't like the way I was changing, and he ridiculed my new way of thinking and acting because my life was radically changing in a good way. I was caught between two worlds, and just before I could decide, I received some news. At the age of twenty-four years, I once again learned that I was pregnant.

Chapter 16

Change Is a Process

Once more, fear flooded back into my life. I was confused and scared, but God helped me choose life. I remembered the harrowing pain I had experienced after my last abortion, and I understood my conscience would never allow me to travel down that road again. I also knew that I not only had the support of my new community, but that I had God's promise that he would never abandon me. I wrote in my journal, "Today, I feel wonderful. I am so happy and filled with so much love inside. Oh, the Lord is good. He has blessed me beyond my belief."

What a contrast from my first pregnancy. Before, I had been filled with anxiety and sorrow; now I was overflowing with love toward the miracle inside me. Shortly after the news, I received a note from Irene that said, "I will be there for you every step of the way." How blessed I was to have friends that cared for me, and how different this was from the isolation I felt as a young girl. Yet, despite my joy at the gift I received, I still worried about the future. Would my child have a father who cared? Would I be able to raise this baby on my own? I never had a mother. How in the world will I manage to be a good mom? That was my greatest fear. You don't know what you don't know. There was so much I didn't know.

It was at this crucial juncture that my life took another unexpected twist. On a bright June day, six months after I received the news confirming my pregnancy, Pete surprised me with a marriage proposal while out to dinner. I was happy and excited, yet confused. Although I initially rejected the idea because I was scared, I soon began to waver. It seemed that Pete had made positive strides in the last few months, and I began to wonder if the news of his impending fatherhood would be the catalyst that finally changed his life. In the end, the thought of a tight-knit family unit, something I had been denied as a little girl, was an opportunity too exciting to pass up, and I decided to accept his proposal.

Although we are called to forgive everyone, that does not mean we are to forget the past mistakes of those we have forgiven. In my zeal for a happy family, I had overlooked the signs that our lives were going down two separate paths. Pete was still living his old way. Do people pick grapes from thornbushes, or figs from thistles? In other words, what you sow is what you reap.

Despite my hopes for our future, it became clear that Pete's transformation was only temporary; he was producing none of the outward acts that characterized a change of heart. Though I pleaded with tears, he refused to renounce the partying and womanizing that had always been ingrained in his lifestyle. Three months after our daughter was born, I made the decision to end our relationship once and for all.

Instead of the isolation and regret I expected to feel as a consequence of my decision, I felt only freedom. So often there are people in our life that obstruct our view of God. It is only when they are removed that we can experience the full power of our divine design. God desires this for all of us.

Chapter 17

A Great Gift from God!

As I approached my expected due date, I felt tense and anxious, and my body was wracked with pain. Lying on my left side incurred soreness in my ribs, and lying on my right side brought heartburn. It seemed that sleep abandoned me the final three months, and I spent many nights lying awake in discomfort. Despite my fatigue, I could barely wait until I was reunited with the child that was moving around inside of me.

I should have expected that my labor, when it finally came, would mirror my life—a hard-fought battle with a few brief periods of rest. I spent about thirty hours in labor from the first contraction, and I'm not sure I would have gotten through without the help of Karen, my best friend, and Pete, who were by my side the entire way. Pete got tired of helping me breathe, so Karen was like a nurse to me; she was making me laugh and cry and just enjoy this whole crazy labor process. Karen could always handle sick, gory, bloody details. She was never afraid of blood, so I knew she was the perfect person to help me through such pain. What a great friend, and to the present day, we are still best friends. It must have seemed funny to the nurses as I yelled, threw up, screamed, and pushed all at the same time. Late in the day, however, it seemed that the battle was drawing to a close. At 6:10 a.m. on September 23, 1995, I gave birth to a beautiful baby girl named Heather Anne Jastrzembski.

The birth of my daughter was the happiest day of my life. My whole world changed from that moment on. God's word says, "A woman giving birth to a child has pain because her time has come; but when her baby is born she forgets the anguish because of her joy that a child is born into the world" (John 16:21). Looking into my daughter's eyes as I held her, I knew that my life would never be the same. I now had a purpose and direction that would sustain me as long as Heather lived. In the days afterward, I would stare in wonder and amazement at this precious little gift God had given me. Heather became the apple of everyone's eye. She was such an angel and my incredible little girl. I felt honored that God entrusted me with this little bundle of joy.

How awesome is the Lord; He sends us blessings from His great love. His mercies are new every morning and His grace is limitless. I now know that "every good and perfect gift is from above, coming down from the Father of the heavenly lights, who does not change like shifting shadows" (James 1:17). He never forsakes those who turn their hearts to Him.

Chapter 18

Sacrifice Is Hard

My strength came from God's abundant love and His word that I always felt like a love letter from God to me, directing my life every day. I was able to start discerning God's still, small voice in my ear, so His word became my journal. I would always underline, highlight, and hear the things God wanted me to know, so I thought I wanted to do the same for Heather. I started a journal of how her dad and I met, how Mom-Mom and Pop-Pop (Pete's parents) met, and the full history of everything I knew of my life and her dad's life, and anyone's life that Heather might need to know about one day. This is something so important to understand. Had I died when Heather was six or seven, she wouldn't remember a lot about me, and she would want to know who I was and if I loved her. Her curious little mind would want to know. She would ask people and friends about me, and she would try to get as much information as possible about me. It would be a huge loss in her life. However, if my best friend Karen gave her the journals of all of my love letters and family history and all the information I recorded in detail for Heather, that would be one of the greatest gifts anyone could receive.

Now when Heather would open the journals, she would feel my love radiate through those pages, and she would know how important she was to me, how much I treasured and valued her, and that she was the greatest gift God has blessed me with. Now, the reason I say this is so important is that that's exactly how I feel about God's love letter to me through His word. I could feel God's magnificent love radiate through every page. That's why I fell so in love with my God, who really transformed and changed my life radically. He taught me to be a radical giver, and you can *never* outgive God. He owns it all. What kept me always getting back up from all my failures and hardships was knowing I *never* had to do it alone ever again. The Lord would tell me often in that still, small voice, "Fear not, nor be afraid, for I am with you where you go." So I *never* felt alone.

The next phase of my life did not get easier. There were financial troubles, depression, the task of homeschooling my daughter, as well as the added challenge of being a single mother. However, God placed on my heart the burden of helping those in need. Over a period of eight years, I took five mission trips to Haiti (three times), Russia, and Nicaragua. At one point, I even drove a school bus and took Heather with me every day to make ends meet, and I became clever enough to introduce myself to all the moms dropping off their children on the bus. I would tell them I was a hairstylist; well, everyone wants to talk about their hair, so Heather and I made friends quickly and I started working at people's houses doing their hair after the school bus was done. It was actually so much fun. I was able to earn money while Heather played with all the kids. I grew a big following in that neighborhood quickly because one neighbor would tell another neighbor and so on. I was a hard worker. I also worked in a salon four days a week in between the bus schedule. Thank God for passion and lots and lots of energy. Those who know me know how much energy I really have. My friends would tease me, saying, "Are you a vampire? You are awake when I go to bed and then you're awake when I wake up. When do you sleep?" LOL! Ancient Chinese secret. I don't need a lot of sleep.

God's heart became my heart. I wanted to give back to hurting little children, for my Lord "comforts us in all our troubles, so that we can comfort those in any trouble with the comfort we ourselves receive from Him." I have learned to rely on the love of God and His support. God's love never fails; it's unconditional and has no bounds. Nothing can separate us from His love. No height, no depth, no width, no length. His love is inexhaustible. God became everything to me—my Mother, my Father, my Grandfather, my Grandmother. He became all the people I needed in life.

Now I wanted to be those things to other kids that didn't have love or support, so I got certified as a foster parent. I took in six different kids at different times through my daughter's growing up years. God spoke to me again in that small, still voice and said, "Kimmy, I want you to love those kids with all your heart, mind, soul, and strength, and give them the love I have given you that they never had." So I did, and it was another incredible journey with each precious foster child I had. They were all unique, special, and precious: Christian, aged six months; Demitri, at three years of age; Kaitlynn, at about ten; Jennifer, at twelve; Stephany, at fourteen; and Lexy, at about seven or eight. I loved them to the best of my ability, and then when it was time for them to move back with their families, I learned to let go when it was time. I knew God would be with them no matter where they would go, and that God would love them and give them the rest of whatever else they needed. I grew in my faith in trusting my God because of His endless faithfulness in every area of my life.

Now, let's get back to a story about my dad. The saying, "Hurt people hurt people, and damaged people damage people" describes my dad. It was not on purpose; it's what he had learned and knew, and he never changed the bad mental programming that he received from his own bad childhood environment and past. My dad was a hurt boy who grew up into a broken, damaged, hurt man. It was never personal. It's that simple. I truly forgave him.

On July 21, 1998, my father passed away from cirrhosis of the liver and Hepatitis B, brought on by years of alcohol and drug use. I am glad to say that we reconciled before his death, and I was able to share the good news with him. Two months before he died, my father accepted the Lord as his savior. Despite the pain and neglect I received at his hands as a child, I came to love and respect him. I found peace after his death, content with the knowledge that his addictions and sorrows had finally been lifted and he was safe in the arms of His precious Lord and Savior.

Another memory that vividly sticks in my mind is after my father had died, I struggled, thinking about if God really forgave him for all the terrible things that he had done. God always meets me right where I'm at. He spoke again in that still, small voice. He said, "Kimmy, I have forgiven your dad for all the bad things that he had done. Now it's your turn to forgive your dad for all the many hurtful things that he had done." So I did, and those were the keys to my greater freedom. The more people I forgave in my life, the more freedom I created for myself. If I would have held onto all the bitterness and pain, I would never have been able to get to the next level of joy in my life.

Without God's love, it would have been impossible to forgive my father for all he had done, but as DL Moody said, "Faith makes all things possible. Love makes it easy." Deep in my mind, I also had the knowledge that I, too, had hurt others because hurt people hurt people and damaged people damage people. We all must understand that God's magnificent love transforms, heals, and restores. He is worth giving a chance to. He is not a Genie in the sky. *He is a real living God who you can go to, and yes, He has boundaries for your well-being. Love says no at times.* If your child wanted to run across a busy street, what would you say? You would say no. He might not understand, but the truth is you just saved his life. Yet, he could think that you don't want him to have fun because that's his perception of it, but it doesn't mean his perception is true. Our children need boundaries, and so do we. There are laws that govern this world that we must live by, like the law of gravity. You can't say, "Well, I just want to jump off this building because I feel like it;" you will have a terrible outcome! Just like the law of cause and effect, there is always an effect of a cause. We create a lot of our own bad consequences because of our behaviors. The hardest person to lead is always yourself. That's why it's so important to know you can go to God for help and power and strength.

Every decision you make creates your life. A positive thought and a positive emotion will always equal a positive result. A negative thought and a negative emotion will always equal a negative result.

Chapter 19

Letting Real Love In

The largest obstacle standing between us and our Creator is usually our own perception. Our subconscious mind that's filled with old and, most of the time, not even true information, is wired in there from our utero state in our mother's womb, and it runs us ninety-five percent of the time. That becomes our autopilot. Now, I started to use my conscious mind and I started wiring in God's loving words of truth, love, forgiveness, and abundant power, and His miracles came to me in avalanches. And God did abundantly more than I could ever have thought or asked for. I have an incredible Maker that I am so deeply thankful for. I could *never* live this life without Him. He has given me one hundred percent potential and I will use that one hundred percent potential for His Glory and my greater good—the greater good of all mankind. Watch for future books where I will share how I've mastered a "miracle mindset."

On August 13, 2002, disaster struck. Pete, Heather's dad, became paralyzed while performing a psycho double jump at Raceway Park in preparation for a motocross event. Pete made a rare mistake and landed the wrong way, severing his spinal cord. Despite emergency surgery and the best efforts of the doctors, the realization set in that Pete would never walk again. He would remain a paraplegic for life.

In the weeks that followed the accident, the Lord began to work on Pete's heart. Pain brings us to our loving Creator. Pete started to pray. He prayed with fervor and intensity, and he allowed everybody and anybody to come see him to pray over him and with him. His spirit was humbled, and he even allowed me to read God's Word to him. Not long after, Pete accepted His loving Creator's Spirit in his heart. What has been impossible for people is possible with God. Although Pete had lost the ability to walk, his heart and soul were restored. Pete had learned to live life differently.

I have come to believe that the worst events in our life always turn out for our benefit. Despite mankind's best efforts, no one can discern the plan of God who numbers the hairs on our head before we are even born. It is beyond our power. All we can do is follow the Spirit of our loving Creator, who leads us, for God always works everything together for the good of those who love Him.

The missionary Jim Elliot summed up the mystery of God's plan. Shortly before his death at the hands of the Auca tribes, he said,

> Granted, fate and tragedy, aimlessness and
> just-missing-by-a-hair are part of human experi-
> ence, but they are not all, and I'm not sure they

are a major part, even in the lives of men who know no Designer or design. For me, I have seen a Keener Force yet, the force of Ultimate Good working through seeming ill. Not that there is rosiness, ever; there is genuine ill, struggle, dark-handed, unreasoning fate, mistakes, if-onlys, and all the Hardy Isms you can muster. But in them I am beginning to discover a Plan greater than any could imagine.

Although Pete's injury had placed him on the path to spiritual renewal, his journey toward the hardship of life helped him grow emotionally in other ways. He has a will of iron to live, and his daughter and family all say Pete has nine lives. He just keeps on ticking, and we call him the bionic man. He drives and still runs his business. He has a very smart engineering mind that keeps him strong. My daughter and I helped get him back to independence in his own life. This was a very hard time for all of us trying to cope with the limitation that now dictated our challenging future. At times I felt that the Lord had called me to assist him in the crushing challenge that he now faced, and by God's abundant grace, I did. Had I not forgiven him for all the pain and hurt he had caused me, I could never have been his friend, or helped nurse him back to life emotionally, mentally, and spiritually.

Chapter 20

Never Give up Hope

One of the lessons I learned as a mother is that children never tire of asking questions. I sometimes wonder where in their life adults lose their wonder for the world, but children never seem to be in danger of losing any of their curiosity. As Heather grew up, she asked me many difficult questions, and I did my best to answer them, but there was always one that made me uncomfortable. On certain occasions she would ask me, "What happened to your mom?"

No matter how much I tried to appease her, it seemed that she was never satisfied with the answers I gave. I told her that I didn't know where my mother was, that the time was not right, and that my mother was very busy. My answers seemed to dissuade her for a time, but that changed when Heather started to attend elementary school. At nine years old, she carpooled with three of her classmates every morning, and one day she returned home triumphant. "I know where your mom is!" she exclaimed. "Joshua told me because he lives right next to her."

I was skeptical that a nine-year-old girl was smart enough to find my birth mom, but one day we drove Joshua back from school to the projects in South Amboy. Heather knew exactly what she was talking about. I decided to check on Heather's hunch and tentatively knocked on the door of 4A. To my shock, there was Bonnie (my mom) standing in front of me. She didn't know she even had a granddaughter, and she warmly invited me in. She acted as if we knew each other for years. I didn't quite know how I felt about all this. We spoke for some time, and I was even more amazed when I learned that she loved Jesus and had many Bibles. I was shocked. It didn't make any sense to me. Why did she not ever try to find me or have a relationship with me? Wonder filled my mind. I had to take this to my Beloved Counselor who I have access to 24-7. He is always available for me day or night.

I said, "Um, well, I don't understand how my mother could know you but not care. All her life she never searched for me. *Why?*"

And then that beautiful, still, small voice spoke ever so softly and tenderly to me and said, "Kimmy, your mom was a hurt person. She lives in shame and regret, and her mental state of mind could not truly accept My love and My healing powers."

I said, "Okay, do you mean, like, 'Hurt people hurt people and damaged people damage people?'"

"Yes, and if they aren't willing to let go of the old thoughts, hurts, wounds, and old patterns that are so deeply entrenched in their mental states in their mind, they can't understand how big My unconditional love and healing is."

So of course, I forgave my mom, and God gave me such unconditional love for her. I stopped wanting and longing for something from her, like wanting her to love me the way I thought a mother should love her child. However, people can't give what they don't have. I left that day happy to just have found her again, and when we got into our car, Heather remarked, "Mommy, your mom really does love you."

Such is God's power to turn even the hardest of hearts. There are no limits to His grace, for he does not show favoritism. He is not far from each of us, and desires that all men come to the truth and comprehend how great and awesome He really is. My mother's conversion is a testament that we are never too far gone to turn back to the truth. Although I never experienced a strong relationship with her, I felt like I had become the mother and she was the child because now I was a much stronger person. I was able to give her the love she had not gotten in her life till now. The Lord's love is so much more powerful than human love. I was able to see her as much as I wanted. However, it was hard because of her lifestyle; I had to put down strong boundaries because of her long-standing abuse of pills and dysfunction. Toxic people can make other people toxic.

She had suffered greatly because of all the wrong choices she made, and all those wrong choices were responsible for creating her not-so-great outcome. I had to learn to let go and love her from a distance. One day I caught her stealing my jewelry, and I was fed up with her crazy antics by now. She covered it up, saying she was just looking through it. I said, "That's it, get all your laundry. I'm taking you home." She never had a car or a license. When I dropped her off, I thought to myself, *Why does she have three bags? She only came with two.* I asked her, "Mom, what's in that third bag?" She had every excuse in the world and said that it was just stuff she wanted to borrow without asking me. So I opened the bag and found all kinds of things like tea bags, dairy creamer, some soup cans, my new beautiful three-piece hat and glove set, and a few of my socks and bras. You could only imagine how mad and frustrated I became. I repeated to her that it's not borrowing; that's called stealing. I cut her off after that.

Two years later, I received a phone call that Bonnie was in the hospital. She had a stroke and it affected her very severely; she was a mess. Well, I was not quite interested in what happened to her. Of course, I went instantly to my Infinite Counselor and said, "Lord, why did they call me? I'm done with her. She has never been a mother to me, nor ever given me even a gift for my birthday. I have never received love, attention, guidance—*nothing* at all from her. She has given me *nothing* ever.

She is a broken, wounded mess and I don't want anything to do with her ever again. I don't care even if she dies."

Now I had to be quiet and still to allow my Infinite Counselor to speak to me. I listened as He said, "Kimmy, I have loved you with My everlasting powerful love and I have given you support and great strength. Now it's time to really forgive your mother for all her wrongs and love her with the same love I have given you."

I said, "*Noooooooooo*. But I can only do so if you give me that love to give to her. I have no more left."

So God filled me up to overflowing and I was able to go see my mom for two years in that live-in nursing home. I would bring her a tape player and food and lie in her bed with her. She would rub my head and say, "I'm so sorry, I'm so ashamed." She couldn't speak properly after her stroke. You see, God works all things together for good. I really believe that was for me, not necessarily for her. I needed her to hold me and love me and speak to me and my heart. I needed that rub on my hair as she would gently caress my hair and say, "thank you" and "I'm sorry." Over and over, she would say that to me, and I needed that even though I didn't think I did. I'm forever grateful that God gave me the strength and power to love my mother the way He wanted me to.

Now, the day came of her intense suffering. I got the call and went to see her. I slept there that night before the Lord took her. I remember that day so vividly. I lay there next to her through the night. She was hot, and by the time I woke up in the morning, she was ice cold. I looked up and said, "Mom, you made it, you're with the good Lord. Now go enjoy eternity."

She looked ahead to a better city, a heavenly one. God is not ashamed to be called their God, for He has prepared a city for them.

My mother passed away at the age of fifty-six. Surely there was much more joy in heaven, for as Jesus tells us, "There is rejoicing in the presence of the angels of God over one sinner who repents."

Epilogue

Happy Endings Are Real

In the years that followed my parents' deaths, I came to understand the challenges of being a parent. In raising Heather, I believe that I have learned as much from her as she has learned from me. Though I thought I had the power to do it on my own, I realized that it truly does take a village to raise a child. I came to rely greatly on Pete's (Heather's dad's) family, not only because our time is limited, but because it's never healthy for a child to receive one perspective on the world. I have become indebted to Heather's dad's family: her father, our friends, her grandparents, her aunts, uncles, and Aunty Karen, my best friend, for all the help they have given in her development. Every day we learn about ourselves, and that process does not stop until our lives are finished.

While many things have changed in my life, it seems that Heather has never stopped with her personal questions. In 2014, after nineteen years of my working at a salon, she said, "Mom, you know, we shouldn't always work for someone else. You should get your own salon."

"Listen, you get a salon, and I will come and work for you," I replied.

Sharon with me and Mark when we were about four and five years old

PETER CONSTANTINEAU
AGE: 45 ♦ SAYREVILLE

Peter C. Constantineau died Friday at Memorial Medical Center at South Amboy. He was 45.

He was born in South Amboy and had lived in Old Bridge before moving to the Parlin section of Sayreville five years ago.

He retired in 1994 after 15 years as a sales representative at R.C. Auto Sales Route 9, Sayreville.

He was a communicant of St. Bernadette's R.C. Church, Old Bridge.

Surviving are his wife, the former Jeanette Clites, two sons, Mark A. and Anthony J., both of Parlin; two daughters, Kimberly A. of East Brunswick and Brittany A. of Parlin; his father, Hank of Sayreville; his mother, Barbara Moran of South Amboy; three brothers, David of Howell, Daniel of Sayreville and John Moran of Florida; four sisters, Donna Baronowski of Howell, Lisa Moran of Perth Amboy, Laura Moran of Parlin and Linda Wong of South Amboy, and two granddaughters.

Services will be 9:15 a.m. Monday from the Carmen F. Spezzi Funeral Home, 15 Cherry Lane, Parlin section of Sayreville, followed by a 9:45 a.m. Mass at St. Bernadette's R.C. Church. Burial will be at Clover Leaf Park Cemetery, Woodbridge.

And this is my dad and Mark my brother and me (Kimmy)

Two weeks later, at church, a man approached me to ask if I wanted to take over a salon. I said no, but he asked me again the following week, and this time, he introduced me to the woman who wanted to hand it over to me. After much prayer and discussion, I decided to accept the gift. Although I didn't have a clue how to own and run a business, in time I learned the ins and outs of managing a company.

Nothing worthwhile in life is easy. Healing and transforming takes awareness and time, effort and energy. Running Modern Tekniques since 2014, I've experienced many tears and hardships. As I successfully emerged out of those trying times, I created my special guidebook, *Simple Salon Solutions*. It's a 112-page guidebook of ten ways that will make and save you time, money, and energy to run a salon successfully. It's on my website, salonsuccessmadesimple.com to purchase. I'm extremely proud of myself for taking all my many failures and turning them into incredible successes. That's how great things are birthed.

I often look back on my life and on the miracle that I am here today. I think about all the people who helped me survive so much of the darkness that surrounded my childhood, and I am filled with gratitude.

One of them stands out above all the others.

Ever since I was a little girl, I prayed to God to help me find the woman who moved in with us when I was about five or six years old, and who helped raise me and my brother and bring us through some of the toughest years of our childhood. Year after year, I asked God to help me find Sharon. I wanted to tell her what had happened in my life—how I had a daughter who I loved, and how I had survived, thanks to her help. For forty-two years, I hopelessly searched for her, but nothing turned up. I was too young to remember all her information and the details of our life, and it seemed that all records of Sharon had vanished. I refused to believe the worst.

Long after I had given up hope of ever finding her, I received an email from a stranger. It said, "Kimmy, I am not sure if you remember me, but I helped your father raise you and your brother Mark. I was going through all my pictures and I came across quite a few pictures of your brother and you. You guys were so cute, and I would love to send them to you and I'd also love to catch up."

This is Sharon and me 2022

As there was no name at the bottom, I was at a loss to determine who sent the email. It was only after I printed out the full email that I found a name: Sharon Vosniak. The words hit me like lightning, and I broke down in tears. After so many years, I had finally found the woman I had been searching for. I felt a flood of emotions. Do I call her right now? I waited to hear from her for so long. She never knew what happened to us, and I didn't want to overwhelm her. There was so much to say, so of course I had to go to my Infinite Counselor, thank Him, cry to Him for all that I was feeling, and just embrace His incredible Love for me. I called her that night and I held back from overwhelming her with too much information at one time. We just picked up where we left off.

She sent me three big photo albums of my brother and me. She had even saved our report cards. Now that's one incredible woman! She gave us one hundred percent of her love forty-two years ago, and those seeds stayed firmly planted for all these years. We reunited and we both cried. It was so good for her to hold me in her arms once again, and the rest is history. We promised that we will continue to stay in touch with each other. I just want to thank my Infinite Counselor (my Lord) who never fails me. One of my favorite prayers in God's word is Chronicles 4:9–10: "Jabez was more honorable than his brothers…Jabez cried out to the God of Israel, 'Oh that you would bless me and enlarge my territory! Let your hand keep me from harm so that I will be free of pain.'" God granted his request. God has granted me my request. Never give up praying.

God willing, in my next book, I will be sharing all of the miracles God, my Infinite Counselor, has performed in my life.

Currently, I am in the process of writing my upcoming book which is aimed at shifting one's mindset and perception to be free of pain, trauma and emotional distress. It is titled: *Reset and Upgrade Your Mind's Software Today*, because you matter.

Acknowledgments

I would like to thank KJ DePontes, who helped me write this book. This book wouldn't even exist had he not been one of my customers and friends. He took on this project and read my countless journals of my crazy, chaotic, confusing childhood and put it in a highly organized script.

KJ was born and raised in Holmdel, New Jersey. If he isn't spending time with friends or family, you can find him engrossed in reading or playing soccer.

Also for Nancy Brito who helped me finish it with all the many countless hours of reading and rereading and editing all the fine details to bring it to completion before sending it to the publisher.

I am thankful to George from Body and Soul for counseling me for the most painful one full year of my life and bringing awareness to me for the first time when I was thirty-five years old. I had no clue about codependency and what it was. Counseling gave me such clarity that I needed in my life to go forward, and programs like AA, Celebrate Recovery gave me support to find like-minded people, so I didn't feel so alone in this big world. I would like to thank Dr. Kilroy (my therapist).

I thank my best friends Karen Holoquist, Marybeth Roberts, Lisa Freeman, Kathy Degregorio, my sister, Brittany Constantineau, my brother, Mark Constantineau and his wife Dianna, my stepmom Jeanette, Mom-Mom, Pop-Pop, and Dolores Mazzeo. These friends and family members have been and still are a strong and loving support system to me.

I am thankful to Andrea Calabretta, who not only helped me get through the devastation of not having a mother but also taught me spiritual healing and wellness.

I thank Lonnie, Cathy Vargas, and Christine, Joe Stocki whose friendship, support, generosity, love, and kindness have been strong anchors in my life.

I thank Jimmy and Christine Loures, who were financially, emotionally, mentally, and spiritually like a family to me; they loved and supported me in everything that I ever did and they still do.

I thank Gerri and Ray Stocki, as well as David Depetro's mother, who mentored me in motherhood for a few years.

I want to also thank Linda Lomez, who was and always is such a good friend. She is also a counselor at Celebrate Recovery, Freehold. She helped me get through codependency and dealing with toxic relationships.

I thank Kim, Erik, and Trevor Traznowski, who supported me incredibly in getting through relationship issues. Kim was an unconditional friend who helped me rebuild the foundation of who I wanted to become.

I would like to thank Karen Biscoff, an amazing outstanding giver, who blessed me with the salon. She believed in me even though she didn't know me. She was financially, emotionally, and spiritually there for me.

I also thank Joan and Bill Zacker, who mentored me at the beginning of my business, who also counseled me spiritually and emotionally to help me get through difficult times.

I thank Dave and Trish Deronde, who had a huge impact on me, who just loved me and supported me like parents. They came alongside me through tough times and painful traumas during my life of being abused, molested, and many other relationship issues.

I thank Mary Sudam, Pasong Schreck who were anchors in my life and wonderful friends.

I thank Jess Stanislowski, who was my assistant for five years and became my steady and stable rock in my life. I just love, adore, and treasure our intimate relationship, friendship, and sisterhood as Christians.

I thank Jessie's parents, Karen and Bruce Koczman, who were there for me when I needed support.

I thank Debbie Brison, an incredible wife of a Christian pastor, who mentored me in the spiritual mindset.

I thank Lorraine & Billy Divizio, Bob Gerber who were my bosses and all the Gerber girls from *Gerber Salon* who quickly became my friends. They were extraordinary influencers in my life for nineteen years, showing me love and support and teaching me to grow consistently and steadily in my craft of hair designing.

I am grateful for all the programs that I took, which helped me get out of the *pit of pain*, most especially for

- The Bible, God's word transformed and woke up my spiritual being my mind and gave me massive wisdom and understanding;

- John Maxwell's online university and all his courses transformed my life and made the shift within the last five years of my life to grow to another level: spiritually, emotionally, and mentally to take responsibility for my life of who I was in the past and who I am now;

- Tony Robbins and Dean Grassio through KBB knowledge business blueprint, Own Your Own Future;

- Bob Proctor and Sandy Gallagher's The Shift, Thinking into Results;

- Mindvalley platform provided limitless classes and courses that gave me greater perception, wisdom (thank you, Vishen Lakhiani!);

- Lisa Nichols, who taught me how to become a professional speaker;

- Marisa Peer from rapid transformational therapy, for teaching me how to overcome the nightmares and bad dreams of my past; and

- Russ Ruffino from COD—clients on demand for taking me to the next greater level of life.

I want to thank all my fantastic customers who have been such a huge part of my journey and healing who have become my friends.

I thank Janet Lenard who was like a second mother to me. She taught me how to make things beautiful in my life.

I want to thank all those who have inspired and helped me grow in wisdom and understanding of what it was to take control of my own life and become one hundred percent responsible for changing my thoughts and subconscious mind that was filled with so much bad programming. I'm so grateful for all these amazing things. I wouldn't be here today if it wasn't for all these people, classes, courses, books, and programs that have helped transform my life forever.

And I especially want to deeply thank Sharon Vozniack for being the first person to show me love and care. My heart will forever treasure her kindness. These are all the pictures Sharon sent to me.

I had to go back to the Kimwood apartments in East Brunswick that once haunted me to face my many demons once and for all. I cried and let it all out, giving myself permission to banish, for good, all of my painful past and to march forward into my Abundant Future.

Kimmy visiting her Childhood apartments
called Kimwood in East Brunswick

About the Author

Kimmy Constantineau is a proud mother, friend, and entrepreneur. Her first passion is loving people, and her second passion is being a life and business coach. That's what fuels her the most. It gives her the most energy and power to do what she does—helping people change their perception to get them past their hurts, habits, and hang-ups to stop living as a victim or a villain and find true healing.

She has learned that it's better to teach a person how to fish than to give them a fish. Her life's purpose is to mentor and influence others for fuller expression and fuller expansion to grow to their highest potential and live a happy lifestyle.

A very special thanks to my daughter, Heather Jastrzembski, who unconditionally loved me in spite of all my dysfunctional ways that she had to live and go through until I got better. She has been and forever will be a solid foundation of *unconditional love* for me. If it wasn't for her, my heart was resistant to change for myself, but for her I was willing to do whatever it took to give her more and better than what I had. Thank God I changed and was willing to never stop changing for both of our greater good.

My daughter Heather Ann Jastrzembski

Me and my girl

Today will never come again

So do something special,

Be a blessing, be a friend

Encourage someone

Take time to care

Let your words Heal, not wound.

Be kind, be gentle,

Forgive quickly

Get filled up with goodness,

Get love and give love.

You only have one life. Make it *great*!